COSMIC
DISCO

*To Kalera and Marcus
and to Lesley and Yansan,
may you find the stars within yourselves.*

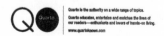

Quarto is the authority on a wide range of topics.
Quarto educates, entertains and enriches the lives of
our readers—enthusiasts and lovers of hands-on living.
www.quartoknows.com

Text copyright © Grace Nichols 2013
Illustrations copyright © Alice Wright 2013
The right of Grace Nichols to be identified as the author of this work
has been asserted by her in accordance with the Copyright,
Designs and Patents Act, 1988 (United Kingdom).

First published in Great Britain in 2013 by
Frances Lincoln Children's Books,
74-77 White Lion Street, London N1 9PF
www.franceslincoln.com

A catalogue record for this book is available from the British Library.

ISBN 978-1-84780-398-6

Set in Warnock Pro

Printed and bound by CPI Group (UK) Ltd, Croydon, CR0 4YY

MIX
Paper from
responsible sources
FSC® C013604

COSMIC DISCO

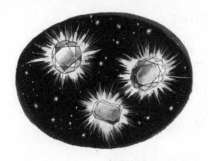

POEMS BY
GRACE NICHOLS

Drawings by
ALICE WRIGHT

F

FRANCES LINCOLN
CHILDREN'S BOOKS

Contents

What Am I?

The gleam within the dream
The ear within the song
The germ within the seed
The eye within the storm

I don't hang around long

A touch of a brain-breeze
A glimpse of a bee's knee
A thought on the wing
A firefly's glow

I make a small light wherever I go

I can come in the sun
I can come in the rain
I can come when you're
Simply gazing from a train

I unlock your creation
My name? *Idea*

Sun, You're a Star

Millions
billions
trillions of stars –
all keeping
their distance

Only you, Sun,
came with your
shimmering dance –
cutting a yellow path
through the dark

My kind of star
cheering us with your glitz
Your autograph –
a flourish of sunbeams
across our skin.

Sky-Artist

Is there no end, Sky-Artist,
to your endless cloud sketches?

Each time I blink you change shape –
a bevy of bears
an army of elephants
a shoal of fish turning sheep

Himalayan pile-ups
so high and deep
we roll in the waves
of a great sea-blanket

Then in a sunny
change of mood
you wipe your canvas
down to its own sky-blue

Soon palaces are floating over me –
a whale lying on a cushiony throne.
Why not a small cloud-dog
to follow me home?

Water, Grass and Dirt

And gazing down
upon his shining handiwork
God, from his heavenly height –
asked an angel passing by one night:

'What's that little old blue ball
spinning in the corner over yonder again?'

The angel answered: 'Why, Lord! that's Earth,
nothing but water, grass and dirt.'

God's eyes lit up like coals of burning ice:
'Sounds to me like paradise.'

Sir Autumn

Sir Autumn is in the garden moving around –
the fallen leaves his cape
of rustling ochre, gold and brown.

Sir Autumn is chuffed to see the branches
of the pear tree weighed down
with firm ripe bulbs;

The apple tree with sweet tinted promises;
the Horse Chestnut spilling everywhere
its conker-jewels. Ah! Such riches.

How Sir Autumn relishes his season's abundance.
But waiting in the wings, Lady Winter thinks –
'It's my turn now, good riddance.'

Lady Winter's Rap

I'm Lady Winter and this is my rap
You'll recognise me by my ice-cap –

By my smoky breath
And my frosty nails
By the nip of my kiss
and my arctic air
you'll realise this gal's got flair –

Cause I'm a cold-hot Mama
When I come into town –
I cloud the trees
I blank the lawn
My days are short
My nights are long
And when I sing, I silence you
With the weight of my song –

By the trail of my cape
And my flakes in your talk
By the bling of my hail
And my slip in your walk
Am telling y'all
Stick to non-slip before ya fall –

Yes, better get out your warmers
No, don't give me verbals
Just reach for your thermals
When I draw near –

I'm Lady Winter and this is my rap
You'll recognise me when my temperature snaps.

Lady Winter's Guest

From behind my window
I spot him coming –
My frosty ways
just don't deter him.
The one they call Robin
No kidding –

Yes, he's got the cheek
to walk down my pristine path
with his Robin-hopping feet
Hopping Robin, tweet-tweet
Hopping Robin, cheek-cheek

But he's the only one
to brave my snow – to venture
my temperature sub-zero.
Gonna make him
my Christmas-star hero –

This Robin-Red-Breast
who dares to warm me
with the flame of his chest.
Stop in, Robin –
I kinda like your hopping.
Be my feathered guest.

Miss Spring

Footsteps returning
as if out of nowhere

Warming earth
with each step of breath –

Spring in her green
and yellow-sleeves dress –

Birds break into chorus
daffodils and crocus come into focus

Sun begins once more to bloom –
Miss Spring, please don't leave too soon.

Summer Mugging

(for Carolyn)

It was a sun-bright summer's day.
Nan took me to Brighton by train –

I licked an ice-cream. She tried a doughnut
as we watched the white-lipped waves.

'Isn't it lovely?' said Nan, lifting the last
piece of doughnut to her mouth –
suddenly a flurry – snatched it clean out.
I couldn't believe it. Nan looked stunned.

While we were caught in a sea-lull
Nan was mugged by a sea-gull.
Summer-mugging happened so fast
Summer-mugging, the memory will last.

A Matter of Holes

The mouse's small open house door
The hidden digs of the spying mole
The fox's Aladdin-den
The miner's descent into Earth's wealth

The woodpecker's hollow
The comfort of our own sleepy burrow
The circle-space behind a guitar's strings
The open-mouth 0 when a singer sings

As for those crab-tracks
Across the cosmic shore
Who knows where they'll take us –
What those black holes have in store.

Moon-Mad

Look at the moon!
A crescent sky-ship sailing
out of a cloudy cocoon

Look at the moon!
A cauldron of amber
spelling, rain-come-soon

Look at the moon!
A Mexican gold plate
over Montezuma's tomb

Look at the moon!
A full-blown O
(I was trying to avoid the word balloon)

Just open the window of your room
and look at the – wolf-raising
sea-swelling shape-shifting
myth-making
Earth-watching moon
holding us
in the bloom of a moon-lock.

Cosmic Disco

Rocking-with-wind trees
waltzing-with-moon ocean –
Everything in purposeful motion
like the lifting lark
or the swirls of Saturn

Even the far-away stars
explode
    on the dance-floor of infinity –
grouping and regrouping
into new constellations.
O see them
    under the shifting disco
of the inter-galactic lights –

The gravitational boys
in their shimmering shirts.
The orbiting girls
in their luminous glad-rags –
within magnetic reach of their rotating handbags.

Borders

Sometimes I do sit and wonder
about our ancient ancestors
who never bothered about borders
who never planted a flag
who never got jet-lagged

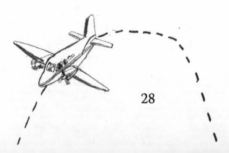

Still-Hip Dad Looks Back

Dad:
I used to break-dance
Turn rippling glass
Stretch my muscles
To the bass –
I used to rip it
And jerk it
And take it apart
I used to chop it
And move it
And groove it

Children:
> *Bet you did, Dad*
> *We can just see those*
> *Eighties-electric-snake moves*

Dad:
I used to wheel it and spin it
Let my spine twist it
I used to shift it
And stride it
Let my mind glide it
I used to ease it
Then just freeze it

Children:
> *We believe you, Dad*
> *Bet you took the shine*
> *Off the floor with those head-spins*

Dad:
You can laugh,
But behind this old
Nine-to-five suit
Hides a heart that
Still knows the route
Back to the back-flips.

Hero Dad

He's never scaled the foothills
of the Himalayas or climbed Mt Everest.

Never parachuted from a plane
or circumnavigated the planet.

Never swam the breadth of any river
or explored the North Pole.

But to his daughter
rapping him up from his deep dreaming
to rid her bedroom ceiling
of that spider creeping by in furtive spurts
sending jiggles down her nerves –

He is a hero all right – a sleepy-eyed knight
mounting that high horse of a stool
a paper napkin his only armour –
See how he catches the eight-legger
and sets it free to weave a safer harbour.

Ancestor-Stars

What is it you're trying to say,
ancestor-stars
when I glance up at you
in the gallery of dark?

Through the eons of time
through the light-years of space
no answer comes back.
Not a single syllable hangs in the air.

Aurora Borealis

Aurora, Dawn Queen,
        Dancing through starlight
In her dress of green
Has to be seen –
        To be believed

Aurora, bending
        Over backwards –
Under the invisible magnetic pole
Pulling in the solar wind
        For her own brand of limbo

Aurora Borealis –
        How she turns and twists –
Such undulating kicks –
An electrical diva
        On the Earth's axis.

Whatever the Weather

As a conversation piece
you can't do better

Whether you're wearing
slippers or leather –

Than simply talking
about the English weather –

Whether it's weather
for ducks or beach-wear

Whether to go out
or curl up in armchair

Whether it's sunshining
or whether it's hail

Whether it's windy
in the Autumn-leaf trail

Whether to coat-up
or whether to cardi

Whether a hoodie
or whether a brollie –

Remember the time you went out
all dressed for Summer

And returned in the evening
on the arm of Winter?

The moral of this tale is –
never get carried away

Whatever the weather forecast says –
Dress for four seasons in one day.

Sonnet to an Earthworm

Earthworm, Earthworm, toiling light
Through the soil both day and night
Does anyone fear your squidgy symmetry
Like the awesome tiger in Blake's poetry?
Or do they just see you as a lowly –
A bait for fish, a meal for birds?
Still you go on tunnelling through the earth
Doing your work – a soft rippling drill
Making spaces for rain and roots to grow in.
Not caring what anyone else thinks
Because you know at least the gardener
And the flowers appreciate your skill.
Earthworm, Earthworm, pinkish-bright,
You help to bring the Spring's delight.

Starlings

How they startle the air
with the wings of their flair

Round

Round the ripples
of pebble-in-pond –
never square or oblong
Round the orange
Round the plum
Round the moon of my Mum's
when-she-was-getting-me tum.

The spinning dervish
prefers the round.
So too the yolk
in the egg that comes.
The comet (though it takes years)
always comes back around
like the seasons' merry-go-round.

Round the planets around the sun –
a well-rounded fire
if ever there was one.
Round the circles
of tree-trunk's girdle
and the flowers that cup
the bees' busy hum.

When it comes to rounds –
Mother Nature knows her onions.

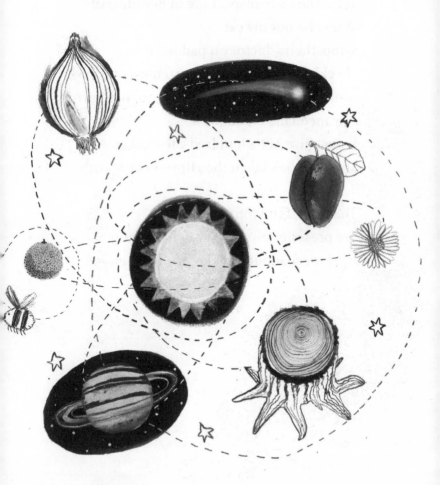

Me and My Cat

Lying in bed, not feeling too well
all curled up like a sea-less shell.
Who comes to inspect me in her fur coat?
Who else but my cat
sympathetic doctor on padded toes
checking me over with her stethoscope nose
soothing me with the apparatus of her purr.
Her medicine is simple,
I must give her a hundred cat-strokes –
after all, she's taken the Hipp-o-cat-ic oath.

That's a cat fur you –
her prescription's always in her favour
but I must admit it makes me feel better.

Which One Are You?

The ailurophile adores cats
The ailurophobe abhors cats

Ailurophile or ailurophobe
Which one are you?

Please form a queue.

Where Do Spoken Words Go?

Where do spoken words go?
Do they have a word-home?

Words of love –
tender and bright.
Words of hate –
hurtful with spite.

Lull-a-bye words
that put baby to sleep.
Deep-comfort words
that can make us weep.

Where do spoken words go?
We just don't know.

One thing's for sure
when words fail
Silence takes our hand.
Tells us a golden tale.

Venus

To the Sumerians –
Lady-of-the-heavenly-Defences

To the Persians –
Mother-of-Fruitfulness

To the Mayans –
She-who-carries-the-sun-on-her-back

To the Greeks and Romans –
Beauteous Goddess-of-Love

(Unasked for compliments
that must have made you blush) –

For when camera-eyed spacecrafts
peered at you closer
they uncovered behind –
the cloudy chrysalis of your dress –
no welcoming butterfly

But a fiery giantess –
Stifling all who ventured closer
with your hydrochloric breath –
embrace a flaming 400 degrees Celsius

But am I bothered, Venus?
Bright-crowned queen of the dawn and dusk.

Reminder of Saturn

My hoola-hooping friend
reminds me of Saturn –
three hoops around her waist
you should see her gyrate –
working up a spellbinding whirl
to keep her rings around her.

New Species

Autumn leaf
blowing in the wind – cat pounces
on new species of mouse

Leaf Man

(Inspired by the painting, Leaf-Man by Lewes artist, Peter Messer)

Born of leaves and dust and air
Leaf-man comes –
Leaf-man who never walks
straight, but drifts through lanes
and quiet passageways.

If you're lucky
you might glimpse him
disappearing down
a path of autumn or veering
round the curve of an alley

Or simply leaning
against an old flint wall.
And when he doesn't
want to be seen, he lets
the leaves of himself fall

Into a golden brown rug –
Then with a swirl
before you can blink
he shimmies himself up
sticking his conker-eyes back in.

Though sometimes he gets
into a spin with the wind –
blown Southerly
when he wants to go Northerly
Easterly when he prefers Westerly.

On bonfire night, he watches
from the hide-out of his hedge,
the dancing flames leap high –
his leaf-nerves standing on edge
when they toss in the guy –

But who knows where he goes
shivering into the darkness?
One thing's for certain –
next year he'll be back again, Leaf-man –
up and rustling to the vein.

The Romance of Sir October
and Lady October

I'm your knight in leafy armour
come to rescue you, Lady October,
from the chilling ills of Winter.

I may not be steel-breasted
but I'm quick-witted –
my style, I might add, is Don Quixotic.

I'm not a dragon-slayer
but where wrong is right, I stand and fight,
my rapier a branch of dappled light.

I am a knight both wise and sober –
note my spurs made of sprigs,
and my medals made of conkers.

I'll cast a gallant cape, if ever
a puddle you should encounter.
Life with me shall be a golden adventure.

Lady October:

O knight in leafy armour, wise and sober
I've already said yes to Lord November.
But give me time and I may reconsider.
That's a lady's prerogative, do remember.

Winter Trees

Gnarled hands
in upward prayer
for green.

Beware-Beware

Beware the shortcut
Beware the maze
Beware the one
With the gobbly-gaze

Beware the dare
Beware the snare
Beware the thread
That isn't there

Beware the glitter
Beware the mansion-gates
Beware the footsteps
You can't retrace.

Making Time

I'm up to my neck
said Mrs Peck

Rushed off my feet
said Mrs Fleet

Missed the deadline
said Miss Divine

Back in a minute
said Miss Fidget

Send me a text
said Miss Flex

My battery is low
said Ms Glow

I'm on Face-book
said Miss Lovelook

Can't beat Skype
said Mrs Snipe

Just follow me on Twitter
said Mrs Glitter

Must make time for me
said Miss Tai Chi

And they all agreed.

Sally Size-Zero

Sally Size-Zero
Sally Size-Zero
Where did she go?
Everyone searched high
Everyone searched low
But could find no trace
Of Sally Size-Zero

Once she used to glow
With a spring in her step
And a sway of her torso
Loved a laugh and a latté
At café Nero
To her friends she was a hero
Until she decided to be a size-zero

Sally Size-Zero
Sally Size-Zero
Where did she go?
Her mother shook out
The bed-clothes to find her –
But couldn't glimpse a wisp or a toe
All that rolled out was a great big zero.

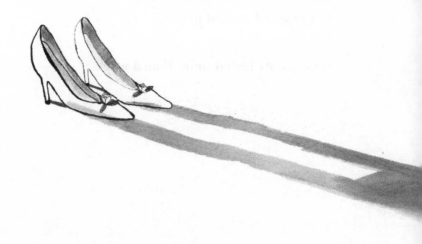

Sweet Nothings

My eyes are like the stars
that illuminate the night

My smile is like a sunrise
that brings your life alive

My speech is like a spell
that turns your ear into a listening shell

My hair is like a magnetic field
that draws you with its flair –

Such sweet nothings you bring
to the small vase of my ear.

If only they lasted more than a week.

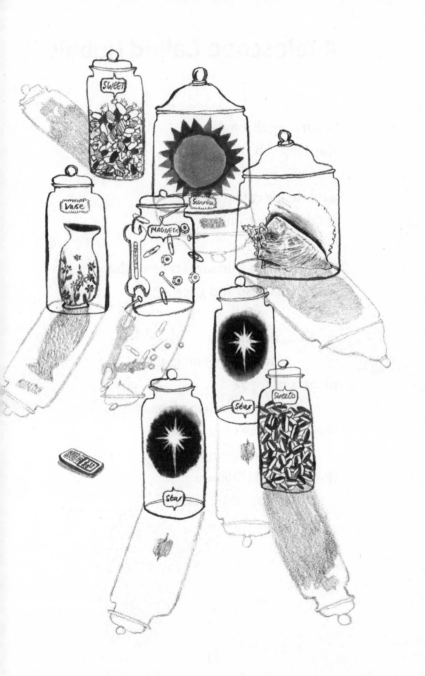

A Telescope Called Hubble

is hurtling through
the deep velvet of space

a telescope called Hubble
is taking the trouble

to beam back a dream-scape of shapes
making us gasp and gape –

cranium moons
        of turquoise and emerald
planets of topaz
        strange mother-of-pearls
the Milky Way's
        diamond-ring swirl
the endless El Dorado
        of stars stars stars –

A satellite shark called Hubble
is taking the trouble
to snap up all the jewels
in the ocean of a vast celestial bubble.

Hummingbird

Hovering in mid-air
like no other –

Forward
backward
upward
then nose
         diving
                  downward–

Iridescent bomber, bringing
no harm to the heart of a flower –

The flower that gives up her nectar
but expects you, Hummingbird, to carry
the golden dust of her desire –

No wonder the ancient Aztecs
named you *'pollinating child-of-the-sun'.*

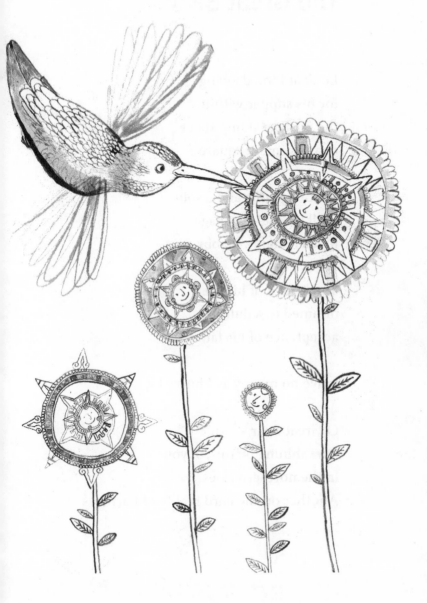

The Great Bear

Look at him, dancing
for his supper within
the postage stamp space
of a pavement square –

A tired shuffle and a spin
is all he could manage
in his hanging shabby coat –

The legend of his eyes
dimmed to a dull
acceptance of his fate.

I give no money as I hurry by.

O Great Bear –
One shining picture of you
in the northern skies.
Another on the hard reality of Earth.

Brian

He was my good friend, Brian,
gentle – a bit shy,
one gold tooth glinting
at the side whenever he smiled.

On school sports day I loved to watch
the notes he made against the high-jump bar –
the way he climbed the air –
his fearless sideways flip. His winging arms.

Until one ordinary Monday morning
our teacher faced us in the classroom –
Brian ... over the weekend ... hospital ...
ruptured appendix ... Peritonitis ...

I remember how I headed for home
blinded by the bright day flipped dark –
and how we took turns bearing his coffin
under a scorching midday sun.

In dreams he's still my good friend, Brian,
laughing, lanky,
a touch of spark,
a floating black question mark.

When The Colours Spoke

Use me, said Green.
I'm essential as the grass and trees
with every shade from deep-leaf to jade.
My emerald green gives hummingbird its sheen.
You can't leave me out of a landscape.

Use me, said Blue.
I am both heavenly and seabreezy.
Indigo, turquoise, lapis-lazuli –
you choose. And isn't it true –
that from outer space our planet is blue?

Use me, said Yellow.
Van Gogh did. Remember
I brought fame to his sunflowers.
Paint me a laughing girl
with a canary on her shoulder.

Use me, said White.
Whenever you need light
I'll be your wide morning
disclosing all the secrets
that darkness likes to hide.

Use me, said Black.
I will add hidden depths.
Keep your shadow-side alive.
I will add a magical mystery
like the stars against the dark of night.

Use me, said Purple.
I am the one favoured by royalty.
In the olden days I was so rare
only rich painters could afford me.
Today you can, so show me you care.

Use me, said Red.
I'm a life-giver with a hint of danger.
Just splash me on. I am your colour.
Like a poppy or hibiscus flower
I will make your painting burn with desire.

Use me, said Pink.
I am more than you think.
You know I always add a healthy glow.
Don't be slow to pick up your blush –
I mean brush – and go Flamingo.

But the painter only said:
No. Today I will use no colour.
Today I will work at a piece of sculpture.

SN2007bi

You were the star that time forgot
in the deepest reaches of the cosmos –

A mega-star mystery
in a dwarf galaxy.

Until one night, telescopic eyes
captured your supernova in the skies –

Giving you fame with a bar-code of a name –
A name you're now stuck with: SN2007bi

If only they'd asked my opinion
I'd have named you –
Firecracker of Mighty Oblivion.

Who Makes Her Own Bed?

Who makes her own bed
and lies on it?

Who plays her own music
and belly-dances to it?

Who designs her own dress but gets
flying-fishes to stitch it?

Who washes and combs her own hair
in her own blue waves?

Who keeps both her jewels and her bones
in her watery cupboards?

Who else but sea – coming to the edge of shore
to lift us off the shells of our toes.

Darkness and Light

Darkness, how I love you, Darkness,
Guardian so kind over our sleep-tight
Keeper of dreams until the moment is right

Light, you're a nuisance
I'm not ready to wake
Remove your harsh face
Give me a break

Light, how I love you, Light,
Revealer of what I need to see and hold
Lighter of paths that bathe us in gold

Darkness, you're a nuisance
You make me stump my toe
Remove your heavy presence
And your gloomy shadow

Sorry, Darkness. Sorry, Light –
Light that becomes Darkness
Darkness that becomes Light.

You

You –

    With the rivers of your arteries
    and the pumping planet
    of your heart

You –

    With the twin-suns of your eyes
    that become half-moons at night
    pulling the tides of sleep

You –

    With the milky-way of your brain
    shooting instructions from your
    follicles to your feet

You –

    with the atoms of a million
    trillion cells –
    A universe yourself.

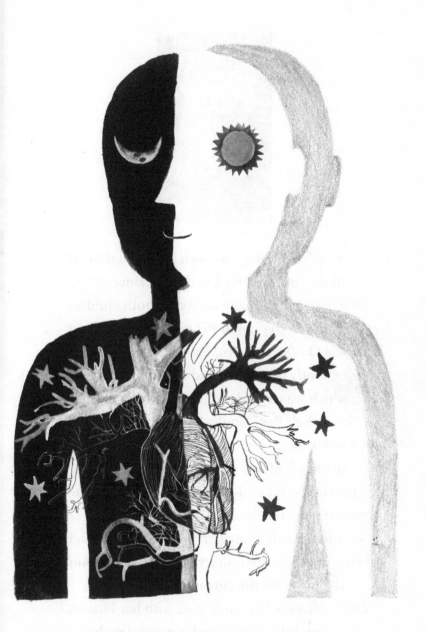

GRACE NICHOLS was born and brought up in
Guyana but has lived in the UK since 1977.
She has written many books for both children
and adults. Her children's collections include:
*Come On Into My Tropical Garden, Poet Cat,
Everybody Got A Gift* and *Paint Me A Poem,*
which was awarded the Children's Poetry
Bookshelf Best Single Author's Collection.
She has also edited anthologies for younger
readers and was poet-in-residence at the
Tate Gallery, London 1999-2000. Among the
awards she's received for her adult work are the
Commonwealth Poetry Prize, the Guyana Poetry
Prize and a Cholmondeley Award. She is among
the poets on the current GCSE syllabus.
Grace Nichols lives in Sussex with her husband
the poet, John Agard, and has two daughters.